TURNING
HOME

SUSANNA TAMARO

TURNING HOME

A Memoir

A Crossroad Book
The Crossroad Publishing Company
New York

The Crossroad Publishing Company
481 Eighth Avenue, New York, NY 10001

Printed in the United States of America

Library of Congress Cataloging-in-Publication Data

Tamaro, Susanna, 1957-
    Turning home : a memoir / Susanna Tamaro.
        p.   cm.
    ISBN 0-8245-1902-7
    1. Spiritual life – Christianity. 2. Tamaro, Susanna,
1957- . I. Title.
BV4501.2 .T2545 2001
248.4 – dc21
                                        2001001425

1 2 3 4 5 6 7 8 9 10   06 05 04 03 02 01

CONTENTS

BEYOND
THE NIGHT

NOT A COLOR
BUT A LIGHT

BEYOND
THE NIGHT

WHEN I WAS A CHILD I suffered from a strange kind of insomnia. For years I was obsessed with the thought that the sun could stop shining. I would look around and see people living in a complete yet blissful ignorance. How in the world could anybody not notice the dangers threatening our planet? How did all these people go to sleep — and really sleep! — with their heads buried in their pillows, unaware of the destructive absence looming around their beds?

Sometimes I would walk around the house with my eyes closed to get used to the darkness. I would touch things and brush up against them. I did this to convince

myself that even in darkness things would continue to exist. However, this was only the darkness of my own little life. What about the darkness of a whole universe?

During those long, dark nights, skeletons would appear before my eyes. They danced sprightly around my room, using the window curtains to mark their stage. They appeared, disappeared, laughing loudly out of their noisy jaws. And they called my name.

That was the reason for my not wanting to go to sleep.

Whom could I talk to about those things? Nobody's eyes seemed to hold the same anxious terror as did mine.

DARKNESS
NEVER ENDING

I knew every minute of the night, and each had its particular noise. Every moment featured a unique form of fright. There was early night, when the children had already gone to bed, but the adults and the building itself had not settled down. I could still hear someone's radio or TV, some arguing voices drowning out the other conversations. I could hear cars passing beneath my window, and beyond the roaring motors, the church bells not so far away ringing the hour.

That was the kind of night that still held possibility. However, there was an invis-

ible boundary. Like actors in a play, the neighbors would disappear into their bedrooms, one after the other. Cars would stop passing, and the interval between the buses grew longer and longer. I heard the breathless uphill drive, the changing of gears, and then silence.

Liquid darkness enveloped everything. Only the ringing bells could still be heard, though their sound failed to comfort me. The skeletons loved those ringing bells; they sang the song to which they minced, on their toes, chanting: "You will die, all of you will die."

If a little girl revealed such fears today, her parents would rush her to a psychologist or another professional capable of using reason and logic to help overcome her anxiety. Fear of darkness is said to be irrational. Skeletons, therefore, can only indicate some morbid pathology.

But is that really true? Or is it our need for security and comprehension that leads us to negate natural human fears? And has not fear been an inherent part of our makeup since the beginning of time?

Sirach said: "A great sorrow has been given to every human, a heavy weight burdens all of Adam's children, from the time they leave their mother's breast to when they return to the mother of all. Their thoughts and their heart's fears are occupied by the coming day of death.... Even when they lie in bed, their night's sleep troubles their thoughts. They sleep very little, as though not at all. They are disturbed in their sleep as they are during the day, because they are devastated by the vision in their hearts, like he who runs from war."

I did, in fact, wake up from my brief tormented sleep exhausted. And exhausted I

15

would feel throughout the day. Rather, the exhaustion itself was transformed into a presence: the presence of death that awaits every creature and carries it into the pits of dust.

The night, the dark, the silence — and the terror that possessed me — were nothing other than a sense of transience. "What is the meaning of living if it all has to end?" I asked myself at that young age. The adults in my life hardly inspired me to ask questions, and there were already too many misunderstandings between them and myself; I wasn't keen on introducing new ones. And the truth is, they had already told me: "You're too much of a loner. That's why you get these absurd ideas in your head."

THE BIRTH
OF DAY

So at night I tormented my older brother.

"When was the sun born?" I asked him.

"And the stars?"

"And why does the sunlight turn on and off on earth like a light bulb?"

"And where do people go when they're not here anymore?"

"And are skeletons good or bad?"

"And will we still be brother and sister when we're skeletons?"

My brother tried, at least for a while, to answer patiently, but then he refused. "Enough!" he said. "Why don't you try to get a little sleep?"

I somehow felt that there was a great mystery in life. A mystery that was being superficially ignored by everyone. A mystery — so I perceived it — which rendered me extremely fragile. For contemplation of any form of life led me directly and without fail to imagine its ending. Those baby kittens I saw would one day die, disappear, just like the cat who was tenderly feeding them. Just like my mother would one day die.

It was impossible to escape from the fact that the future was full of pain.

So if there is death, what is the meaning of life? Why is there life at all?

"Our lives are brief and sad. The remedy is not in man's hands, nor is it known by those who have returned from the other world. We were born by chance, and when we die it will be as though we never existed: the breath in our nostrils will be smoke, and the word a spark in our beating hearts. Extinguished, the body turns to ash and the spirit disperses like light air." These are words from the Book of Wisdom in the Bible. Words that may easily be perceived as coming from a nonbeliever. The person who does not believe is unable to see the mystery. All that exists is consumed in the moment, because all moments have their end, and we must grasp them, before they disappear, taking us with them into nothingness.

Jean Paul Sartre wrote: "Death is never that which makes sense of life, but that which takes its meaning away." This could be the epigraph of modern times. Those who do not believe have to negate the mystery of our origins. Atheism not only negates God; it also ends up having to negate the human person. When we extinguish the mystery of the human person, we reduce ourselves to a two-dimensional silhouette, an extremely limited and poor form of existence. Perhaps it is precisely that extreme limitation which creates pride and presumption: we see a small slice of reality — or of existence — and we confuse the slice with the whole pie.

AMAZEMENT
CATCHES
THE LIGHT

Aristotle said: "Amazement is the principle of philosophy." But people today are rarely capable of being amazed. On the contrary, this obvious sign of inner poverty is loudly advertised and filled with a new credo: "God is dead and humankind is finally free.... We are nothing but relatives of the apes.... Chance determines everything.... Good and evil don't exist; they are just relative values." Such ready-made thoughts have become the unquestionable essence of our culture.

22

How is it that we have become so astonishingly numb?

Why are six- and seven-year-old children turning into little presumptuous and indifferent sceptics? Able to explain almost everything, they are often entirely incapable of experiencing that brief tremor which is genuine amazement.

I believe that this condition comes from the certainty that we have all the answers, that everything can be understood and explained according to the precise laws of cause and effect. Each action causes a reaction, and the reaction then catalyzes a new action. In this chain of events, there isn't room for mystery nor any space for surprise.

And yet, all you have to do is to observe a single day of life, any life, with open eyes and a free mind. You will realize that really everything holds a surprise. And often it is

24

the unexpected that disrupts the schemes of order.

The second step of my journey was precisely this: astonishment. The answers from scholastic instruction had failed to satisfy me.

FLOWERS BREAKING THROUGH CONCRETE

At the age of seven or eight, I began to look around myself. The more I saw the more questions flooded my mind. Walking along the street, I saw weeds breaking through concrete sidewalks. I saw them grow and flower. I saw insects and butterflies poised on their corolla. I watched them survive under the feet of the people passing by, in the midst of exhaust pipes. I asked myself: "What gives them their power? This extraordinary power that allows them to break through concrete. Why do they not only grow but offer the world their little blossoms?

Watching nature I became more and more fascinated by all that went on. And the more distant the skeletons grew. They became the memory of a frail age, when it is not yet possible to conclude anything from what goes on around you. The colors and forms of nature slowly absorbed my sensibilities, overwhelming the darkness of my insomniac nights.

Later on, I felt a frenetic desire to know, understand, and classify. I had no interest in poetry, stories, or literature. The only thing that interested me, in an obsessive way, was nature, the richness of color and the various forms of existence.

THE TREASURE
OF VARIETY

The variety and the richness provoked in me — and still does — a continuous surge of amazement. Imagine the brightly colored hummingbird, or parrots that live in the tropics, the lyre birds, the large Amazon butterflies. If you think of them, it seems apparent that the first gift of creation is beauty, a beauty marked by uselessness. Isn't this an invitation to be amazed? If everything were only about cause and effect, then how to explain sheer beauty? And what about the endless variety of forms in which this beauty manifests itself? What is beauty telling us?

BEAUTY IS A FUNCTION
OF LIGHT

Besides being gratuitous — way above and beyond its evolutionary function — beauty has a fundamental characteristic: It exists only as a function of light. It is light that catalyzes hormones that incite the mating of species at the proper time. Light makes the hummingbird's plumage emerald green. It is light that allows us to see an infinite variety of things with our own eyes.

"Let there be light" are words of the book of Genesis. "And there was light. God saw that the light was good, and he separated the light from the darkness."

31

Obviously beauty — and life's unpredictability — are still before our eyes. But perhaps we are no longer capable of seeing them. I used to love taking long walks alone when I was a teenager. I liked to climb mountains or walk along the seaside. I felt as though the grandeur of the open horizon referred in some unmistakable way to the might of whoever created the universe. Yet in that very vastness was the risk of getting lost.

And perhaps it was this fear of losing myself that spurred me to examine not just the small but the minuscule.

THE WHALE HAS
ITS OWN DNA

In my last novel, *Anima Mundi,* Sister Irene says to Walter: "Look at these little seeds. Look at how unattractive they are. They are absolutely ugly. If you didn't know what they were, you could think that they were some little rodent's excrement. And yet everything is in here, in these percentages of a square inch. There is compressed energy and a growth plan. The large green leaves that shade the earth in June are already in there. Many people are moved by great open spaces — the mountains or the ocean — it is the only way they are able to feel part of the living, breathing earth.

But for me, it is the opposite. The tiniest of things give me a vertigo of the infinite."

Such vertigo of the infinite becomes immediately apparent when I consider the base materials, the physical and chemical elements of life. How could it possibly have been accidental when the fist macromolecules linked together in the primordial swamps? And how could such a simple molecular structure create the double helix of protein and amino acids that formed — and form — all existent species?

The whale has its own DNA, just as the sea horse does, and the tiny threads of the copper butterfly and the oak tree. And so do human beings.

Every man and woman has a DNA uniquely theirs. And many things are inscribed in that thread: grandfather's voice, great-great-great-grandmother's eye color, another person's height, the shape of another one's hands, a talent for math rather than an artistic inclination, temperament, a predisposition to a certain illness, and many other things that we still do not know.

Our DNA is the broad outline of our lives, and inscribed within it are the many roads we may choose to travel. "May," not "will," for I am convinced that our genetic makeup is simply an indicator of our life, and that it is up to us, our conscience and our will, to choose the best and highest path possible.

WILL CREATES ORDER

How can we not see a plan in the uniqueness that bears our name? And in bearing our name, are we ourselves not made bearers, and wielders, of a mystery?

This mystery — the mystery of life — is an even bigger mystery than death. The fact that we are here, that we have been "called" to exist, is more powerful than chaos in the universe. I am almost tempted to say that when we are alive death ceases to exist.

CAUSE, EFFECT, AND MYSTERY

The current trend is to attribute everything to chance. But does chance exist? Things that happen by chance happen without a plan. Two molecules bond "by chance," just as two people meet "by chance," and "by chance" this union may enable another living human being to be created who "by chance" will have grandma's blue eyes and will love botany like her great-great-grandfather.

Chance means that everything ends up being attributed to lucky circumstances. There are no plans, no choice, but rather an inevitable chain of events that, oddly

enough, repeats itself with absolute perfection since the beginning of time.

I am a very messy person. If I do not apply my will, the space around me will turn into true chaos in a very brief span of time. Therefore, if I leave things to "chance" in my room, I will automatically and unconsciously create a mess. To transform it into order, I am forced to make a choice, to perform a conscious act: zoology books in one place, colored pencils in another, T-shirts into a drawer, and jackets into the closet. In my case, therefore, chance creates disorder and will creates order.

It seems quite evident that in our universe there is order.

In Hebrew, the language of the Holy Scriptures, the word "chance" does not exist. In Italian (*caso*), it is derived from the Latin word for "to fall," just like the English word "accidental." Falling, then, indicates a movement from higher to lower, according to the laws of gravity. It is not a horizontal movement; one does not fall from right to left or from East to West.

In the 1500s Pietro Bembo reflected on chance, which he called "causes for human action, mysterious and sunken in time." Mysterious and sunken in time — something, indeed, that we do not know, and that exists prior to us.

In the end, then, "chance" is just another word for "mystery." But as opposed to mystery, the word "chance" appeases our conscience, and enables us to feel exceptionally smart in that we have liberated ourselves from the chains and prejudices that held human creativity captive for centuries.

If everything happens "by chance," what do my choices mean? Why would I work to develop my talents and strengthen my potential? If we were tossed into life "by chance" and swept away "by chance," what is the sense of doing anything in the short time span between birth and death?

A life lived "by chance" is a life suspended between boredom and the anxious expectation of its end. It is free merely on the surface, because true freedom is to feel free from the dread of death.

When we cease to encounter new horizons that lead our lives to grow, we grasp onto the less important things of life, things that promise, if just for an instant, to offer us roots: success, money, sex, power.

Modern life is dominated by fake values, and at times people make great sacrifices to comply. But living in this dimension means that we have to become detached from ourselves. And detachment is a dead-end street.

Those who live completely detached

from their inner dream are blind, dancing around time without ever arriving at the essence of their being. That can lead only to disappointment.

What kind of life is that? Is it a continuous race for a goal that in the end proves to be worthless? "Vanity of vanities," says Qoheleth, "everything is vanity." Is it not vain to feel superior to mystery or to judge it as far too simple an explanation?

NOT A COLOR
BUT A LIGHT

ONCE I WAS INVITED to speak about justice and forgiveness, and I felt a little insecure about that topic. I am by nature insecure, and every time I begin a new task I mistrust my own ability. My inner voice keeps saying: "That isn't for you; you can never do that."

That time the voice was even stronger: "Do you think you're a legal expert?" No. "A theologian?" No. "Ethicist or philosopher?" No. "Are you at least a murderer ready to repent?" Not even. "Then don't take the assignment. You'll just embarrass yourself to the bones. Cancel it at once!"

Over the years I had learned not to listen to this inner voice as much, but that time

it seemed to have a case. How could I talk about such a daunting issue without a long period of preparation?

Writer are in a strange position. We know lots of things about lots of things, but nothing sufficiently to speak with authority. We have no academic achievements to show. No degree or diploma that could certify our knowledge.

Ours is a strange state of wandering. We go here and there. We take a little something here, let something lie there. But no matter what, we keep on going like a cheerful dog following an invisible scent.

In the end a book is born, something that did not exist before. Rarely does a novel reflect structured knowledge or a one-dimensional view of the world. Rather it portrays life's complexity, fluidity, and profundity. And with a little luck, life's poetry as well.

SPEAKING OF RECONCILIATION

As I thought about this, I came to realize that there was a reason for inviting me to talk about justice and forgiveness. Practically all of my books, those for adults and children alike, speak of reconciliation.

"In forgiving, we are forgiven, in dying, we are given new life," says St. Francis in a simple prayer that I quoted at the end of the novel *Anima Mundi*.

Through all of my literary work I have walked the long path that leads to reconciliation. But strangely enough, until that invitation to speak, I had not noticed this clearly.

WHERE THERE IS DARKNESS

When I realized that I was able to write, I understood that the ease with which words and thoughts flooded into my mind was not meant just to paint flowery landscapes. I was called to clear a path into the forest. I wanted to get to the basis of knowledge. To go way down where there is darkness and try to shed some light. Though I have never formally studied philosophy or theology, I felt the need to scour, to go to the bottom, to reveal the hidden things of life.

Even as a young child before I went to school, I had this desire to dig down deep. I watched the people around me and sensed

a certain kind of suffocation: They were sad, unhappy, and resentful. But I never understood why.

While I felt such joy and sunny happiness, around me I often noticed confusion and depression. In the simple world of my little heart everything seemed so clear: an immense light of love dwells within us; we just have to follow it. Or better: we should follow it. Because no one seemed to do so. Why did adults never seem to do so? Why had their lights flickered out? Or had they never shone at all? And above all: why so much pain?

A LAND FILLED
WITH HATE

I grew up in a land filled with hate, at a time when the acrid clouds of smoke had only too recently evaporated. The soles of my feet sensed the tremor of the earth. I felt an unbearable tension in the air that my eyes could not see: people living estranged from themselves, either reacting excessively or closing up in apathetic silence.

At the time, of course, I knew nothing of history and the horrors that had taken place in those few square miles. Just like I knew nothing of Jesus, salvation, or the Holy Spirit. But somehow I felt, in the innocent profundity of my infantile soul, that

a person's life meanders along deviations rather than following a straight path.

All around me was constant talk of war. Of "The Big One," in which my grandfather fought, and of the Second World War with its bombings, its deportations, and its deathly madness. If the First World War was "The Big One," then the second had to be smaller. But according to my grandfather's stories, the second was even more frightening and bloodier than the first. And that wasn't the end. If there had been a First and a Second World War, then there would surely be a Third and a Fourth World War, so that, in all equality and justice, each generation would have its own epochal calamity.

This confrontation with cruelty and death has accompanied me since early childhood. I thought a lot about evil and hatred, about the devastation that occurs in people's lives, and about the possibility of interrupting the circle of violence. I also thought about indifference, because it is the main road to destruction.

On Sundays my grandfather used to bring his grandchildren on a pilgrimage to the battlegrounds. We picked primroses and cyclamen on fields that had once been flooded with blood.

Hidden under the grass you could still find the trenches and the tunnels connecting them.

"This is where I was wounded," Grandfather told us on one of our outings. "And there we fought the enemy face to face." His words held neither rhetoric nor hatred. He happened to have been a soldier. And if he had committed his share of cruelties, he did not speak about them. War, to him, was something sad and horrendous that he hadn't been able to escape.

Yet beneath the hot earth a million dead people lay, killed in the big battles of two wars. And there were the pits, large natural hollows into which hundreds and hundreds of human beings had been thrown, many still alive. I always walked quietly across that field so I wouldn't disturb the silence of the dead.

"The pits are filled to the top," my brother said, knowing how easily I could be impressed.

I knew that a distant cousin was in there. They took her from her home and brought her here, into the pit.

"Why?" I asked one day.

"Because of her political beliefs," someone answered.

That is how I came to understand the unimaginable tragedy that dwells in the creases of our history.

THE COACH WITH
DARKENED WINDOWS

And then I discovered that evil searches out all sorts of other cruelties as well: hatred, for example, pure, ferocious hatred, person-to-person hate, hatred directed at members of ethnic groups or simply at people who have different ideas. But hatred destroys. It makes fathers and sons, siblings and friends from childhood days kill each other.

More and more the presence of evil took up room within me. Like an eclipse blackens the sky, all other thoughts were taken over by the tyrannical concept of evil.

I kept telling myself that there was an

evil principle governing the world. Like a
worm it devoured hearts and minds until
they dried up, emptied out, got lost. The
few who seemed to have decided for the
good were destined to succumb.

I told myself that there was no salvation
from the principle of evil across the world,
and maybe even the skies were blank.

Contemplating evil results in atheism,
doesn't it? If God is love, where in the
world can love be found? God made this
world. If God is indeed good and com-
passionate, how can he allow this mad
destruction?

At this point people may cease their
questioning, having decided that God does
not exist or is too unjust to be taken
seriously. I, too, might have continued
to contemplate my disappointments. But
something called me to move on. To stay at
the level of resentment would have meant

to make the rest of the journey of my life in a coach with darkened windows.

It would have become a journey of inner impoverishment and lowly emotions.

Something of what had given such intuitive certainty to the little girl was still alive within me. It sparkled like a flame, small, but by no means weak. Stubborn, and not at all willing to be extinguished.

The answers I had been given in Sunday School couldn't satisfy me anymore. I felt treated like a fool, placated with clichés and pat answers, like in some stupid television talk show.

No one was there to walk with me or to direct my search. "Why don't you go out and play instead of asking big people's questions?" I was told.

ON REALITY AND
ON THE TRUTH

But I wanted the truth. I was searching for the truth of my life, the truth *within* my life. I demanded a truth that would let me understand the truth of all other life stories as well.

Yet only a little later in my life I was informed that truth didn't exist at all, but that there were about as many truths as there are women and men. My search for one truth was considered naïve and senseless, an infantile characteristic, so to speak.

Reality, I was told, is above all else an expression of a highly complex system: structures and metastructures — truly a

labyrinth in which one could easily get lost. More so, where one would have to get lost. Intelligence is measured by the ability to navigate through this endless multiplicity of life's hypotheses, without ever accepting any of them.

When we enter adolescence we are very fragile and insecure, afraid of being rejected or considered stupid. So I too made an effort to conform to such reduced perspectives of reality. Though I wasn't very successful.

The same people who disputed things with such eloquent intellectual confidence sensed the same deep pain that had tortured me during my childhood; I could tell. There was something incomplete about their journey; their actions testified to a confused indifference. They spoke of chance as if they were the lords of it; and cynicism was called the emotional litmus test. They moved around a low and dark horizon trying to direct everyone else's thought into a confined space. Different ways of thinking were laughed at, and there was a sad ability to block every nonconformist idea at once.

Judging others was a favorite game. But every judgment carries traces of contempt.

In those years of inner chaos I never stopped believing in God in spite of the disappointments I had experienced in catechism class. I did not know yet what face this God wore; I was too obsessed with the presence of evil. But anyway, wherever I went I carried the gospel with me. Time and again I opened it for advice. I was determined to get to the bottom of truth.

Eventually I got to a point where nothing within me corresponded anymore to my surroundings, or to anything that happened to me for that matter. My life was unfulfilled, and I couldn't bear it. I retreated to a small village in Israel to be far away from everything and everybody, and to meditate.

BLOOMING INTO SILENCE

In a short time my mind blossomed into silence and solitude, and without effort I recovered the unique mind-set of a little girl: radically driven by the joy of living each moment.

There in the village I experienced the absolute presence of the Holy Spirit, with every fiber of my body and my soul.

At that time I understood: The heart is the center of all things. And my heart was — as it may be for most people — bogged down far too long with all kinds of ballast: the ballast of my ignorance, my inner chaos, my becoming more and

more estranged from myself and my own life.

But suddenly truth revealed itself with an absolute brilliance. And everything, however small, was bathed in its clarity.

BE RECONCILED
WITH YOURSELVES

Now what does all this have to do with forgiveness? I had to leave evil and hatred behind me in order to experience grace in all its grandeur.

So what about forgiveness?

Often we think of forgiveness as something we offer those who have hurt us in serious ways. Obviously, that is one of the noblest forms of forgiveness.

Perhaps we consider forgiveness an indulgent duty to be fulfilled after another person has made a mistake, the sort of sugar-sweet superiority demonstrated by believing Christians as they practice the

virtue of offering an enemy the other cheek.

All this, I think, is not yet true forgiving. It is more like the parody of a feeling that is much richer and more complex.

We rarely think of forgiveness as something we have to extend to ourselves.

When Frère Roger Schutz, the esteemed founder of the international and ecumenical Taizé monastic community, stood before the hundreds of thousands of young people who had responded to his invitation to a Pan-European youth prayer summit, he called them to reconciliation: "Be reconciled with yourselves; be reconciled with your childhood. Without reconciliation there is neither freedom nor love."

He is so right. I think that the word "to forgive" is the key to a more comprehensive understanding of life.

NO NEED
FOR DEFENSE LINES

But what exactly does it mean to forgive?

Forgiving is a long journey that begins with the acceptance of our weaknesses and our history, whatever they may be.

It is the only journey that empowers people to be free truly and to love deeply.

A reconciled person, someone who can forgive, is above all else a person who needs not put up lines of defense and barriers. This person knows that the truth is never exclusively white, and never just black.

People who have been reconciled with themselves can see that the truth is not a color but a light. It is a bright light

that shines everywhere, spreading warmth and clarity and making visible the splendor of even the littlest of things. I believe that reconciliation is not a show of human goodness. Rather, to forgive is a long and arduous process of stripping ourselves of our egotism. But in the end we will become fully human and fully ourselves, able to live the life we desire in fullness.

THE PRODIGAL SON

I have always cherished the parable of the prodigal son, and I find myself using it in my books again and again. It is one of the gospel's most famous stories. But as it happens with many things we have heard so often, we seldom take the time to really listen, and thus we miss the meaning of the words we remember so well.

The story has been told many times: There is a son with no discipline or decency, one of those who have lived at all times in all places. One day he calls on his father demanding his inheritance. He moves to a faraway land to seek his destiny. But things don't go well at all, and

after a short while he has to return home and offer his services to his father in order to survive.

The father, whom we might expect to slam the door in his son's face, instead welcomes him with open arms. In addition, he throws a big welcome-home party, not letting himself be distracted by the jealousy of the son's older brother, who, faithful to tradition, has stayed home and worked obediently with the father all along.

At first sight, this story is so simple. However, I find it to be a powerful metaphor for our times.

FREEDOM
THAT I MEAN

During the past two centuries humankind, with an unprecedented boldness, has separated intellect from love. In the arrogant euphoria of a vast new scientific knowledge we set off to make ourselves the craftsmen of our destiny.

Freedom has become one of life's fundamental values, yet we got stuck in a freedom that directs itself, and we lost our orientation.

To free oneself of one thing usually means to become the prisoner of another.

Instead of a people intimately and profoundly free from the inside out, we have

become the slaves of our own concept of freedom.

Gradually we have freed ourselves from everything: from taboos and limits, from doubts and anxiety, and most of all from all that reminds us of moral laws. In addition, we have freed ourselves from the seemingly antiquated and oppressive concepts of God's existence. Now we can live with the certainty of being the sole managers of our future.

Modern history, however, has revealed this to be a fallacy. The empty skies are not being filled with the grandeur of humanity, but with its madness, its pride, and its terrible thirst for blood.

The freedom we won by shedding ballast and responsibility was ill conceived and is showing its frailty. We have lost respect — respect for ourselves, respect for others, respect for the world around us.

WE ARE
A HURT PEOPLE

Today we are a hurt people. Troubled deep within, weakened beings, crushed between the inability to live in the present and our constant anxiety about the future.

We suffer an acute kind of "infantility." While lacking the abundant joy of child-likeness, we show an infantile childishness featuring the most egomaniacal vanity.

Like the younger son of the parable we have received talents from the father — in this case, our intelligence. Humankind has traveled far to take its destiny into its own hands. But there is no denying that all sons

Susanna Tamaro

and daughters are intrinsically connected with their roots.

The theme of returning is dear to me. It is the road on which Walter and Andrea embark in my book *Anima Mundi*. Andrea, incapable of going all the way, confronts Sister Irene with this parable, and she later speaks of it to Walter: "That evening, after dinner, I showed him the parable of the prodigal son in the gospel. He read it more than once to me, and then he said:

" 'But that's not just.'

" 'What's not just?'

" 'That the son who acts righteously is treated with indifference and that a big party is thrown when a delinquent comes home. Why don't the others object? Why don't they throw him out, tell him to go back where he came from? What does this mean? That it is best to act badly?' "

Andrea responds like the son who stayed

88

faithfully at home and like all those who don't feel loved enough and who envy the light that they see shining in others. "Listen," says the older brother, who stayed home with his father, "I served you for many years, never disobeying you, and you never threw a party for me and my friends."

His reaction is understandable and quite normal. It corresponds to the emotions of people who never risk anything in life, who never put all their eggs in one basket, but rather stick faithfully to what is certain, the rules, the things expected of them. This may be considered an achievement, though it may just express a fear of life. And certainly it doesn't earn the right to judge others.

This is precisely the arrow that pierces your heart in the parable. There are so many older sons among us. The human soul is quick to embark on the road of duty instead of the path of love.

Duty doesn't necessarily make for an easy life. It is boring; everything is constantly repeated. And yet its attraction lies in the certainty and relative security it offers. All one has and all one gives move within a set framework. Those who do not act, yet judge, are no better than those who risk and lose in order to find their own way. And those who boast, drunk from their personal balance sheet, show no more than a personality that is not free and unable to open up, to listen, and to understand.

Understanding is born when we fall and experience our own frailty, when we live through times of defeat and learn to accept them. Resurrection requires death. Death to arrogance. And death to concepts that attempt to create destiny outside the law of love.

The obedient brother, the victim of jealousy and hatred, is destined to immobility and a life behind the closed doors of his emotions. That way he can never get to know the gift of absolute freedom that flows from the spirit of reconciliation. As much as he judges others, a man of justice he will never be.

Justice is an attitude gained in the course of a lifetime and through the understanding of one's own path. One acquires an ability to grow from obedient slave to son or daughter. Then others become siblings.

Those who limit the imagination of their life's potential to the alibi of "doing-what-everybody-does" are incapable of understanding the nature of the human spirit as it oscillates between the need for strong certainties and the desire to overthrow the past.

Only by acknowledging our own limits

and our frailty can we move beyond mere obedience to a freedom that allows us to commit ourselves spontaneously to a love that fully accepts its responsibility.

NOTHING LEFT
TO LOSE

Sadly, the older brother never understood that he himself is in need of forgiveness. He needs to understand his dilemma, and he needs to forgive himself.

But in order to understand ourselves, we need to know ourselves, we need to accept our emotional limitations as well as our fear of freedom.

The process of reconciliation begins when we experience our own limitations and weaknesses — in regard to our own life and in relationship with others. This is the only space where justice can grow.

Reconciled persons have completed the

path of spiritual self-realization. They shed all that only serves the ego and give up all that may make them less than equal or more distant from others. When everything is lost, there is nothing left to lose.

A truly reconciled person no longer exhibits pride or arrogance, but is completely available for love.

"Love's logic is a sort of nonlogic" says Sister Irene to Andrea in *Anima Mundi*. "Often it follows a path that is incomprehensible to our intellect. There is a gratuitous nature to love, and this is what we cannot accept. With normal logic, everything has its value and its price. Actions, as seems clear to everybody, are followed by reactions. Effects need causes.

"God's love is different. God's love is without measure. Instead of fixing something it may turn everything around. That, of course, is startling and also frightening. But that is exactly why the younger son can return home to find not anger, but overwhelming joy.

"He has made mistakes, he was confused, maybe he even has done evil things. But then he returns, not accidentally but on the basis of a decision.

"The son decides to return home to the father's house."